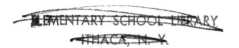
Fingerprint Detective

ROBERT H. MILLIMAKI

J. B. LIPPINCOTT COMPANY/PHILADELPHIA AND NEW YORK

To my wife Joan

16 O   1 U OOO 14
M 17 U OI I

for her patience, understanding and
encouragement; and to those future
fingerprint technicians who will some day
devise newer and better techniques.

I would like to thank the Federal Bureau of Investigation for providing
many of the photographs used in this book, and for the training which
made this book possible, particular thanks to special agent, Tom Burg.

Robert H. Millimaki

U.S. Library of Congress Cataloging in Publication Data

Millimaki, Robert H.
  Fingerprint detective.

  SUMMARY: Traces the history of fingerprints as a means of identification and describes
how fingerprints are located, developed, lifted, classified, and analyzed.
  1. Fingerprints—Juvenile literature. [1. Fingerprints. 2. Criminal investigation] I. Title.
HV6074.M47   364.12′5   73-7861
ISBN-0-397-31484-1 (reinforced bdg.)

Contents

1   **Rolling Prints**

The woodsman kneeling to study the track of the timber wolf, and the fingerprint technician examining a set of fingerprint cards, are both hunters of exciting, elusive quarry. But if the woodsman is wrong he may wind up trailing "Rover" to his dog house, instead of the timber wolf. He might feel a little silly, but that's all.

A fingerprint technician can't just shrug off an error because it can mean the difference between life and death. He has to be correct in his judgment.

Fingerprint identification isn't the puzzling mystery it might appear to be. The secret lies in knowing what to look for, where to find it, and what to do with it when it is found.

There are two good ways to go about solving a mystery. One is to ask someone who knows the answer. The other is through experimentation. Experiments not only show you the answer, but they're a lot more fun.

Since an experiment is just another way of asking a question, first you have to form the question in your mind. Then you can set up an experiment to discover the answer. Thinking about fingerprints, some questions that might come to mind are:

What is a fingerprint?

Are everyone's fingerprints really different?

How does a detective find fingerprints he can't even see?

Could I find a fingerprint and identify it?

We could go on and on with the questions, but let's set up a simple experiment and try to answer the first one: "What is a fingerprint?"

Since observation plays such an important part in the science of fingerprints, let's start by testing your powers of observation. Look closely at the skin on the tips of your fingers. Now, look at the skin on the back of your hand. Do you see any difference?

If you observed a pattern of lines on the tips of your fingers, and noticed that the back of your hand was smooth, you're right. This lined pattern is called *friction* skin. It's nature's way of helping us to grasp and hold onto smooth objects.

As you can see, the lines are not only on the tips of your fingers, but on the palms of your hands as well. There is only one other place on your body where you will find this kind of lined pattern. If you guessed the soles of your feet and toes, you're correct again.

If you were to look closely at your fingertips under a powerful magnifying glass, you would see that the lines are formed like the rows in a plowed field, with ridges and furrows. In fact, these lines are referred to as ridges, and the depressions between the ridges are called furrows by the technicians who work with fingerprints.

To actually see how these ridges and furrows form various patterns, let's go on with our first experiment. The only materials you will need are a clean sheet of paper, an inked stamp pad or, if a stamp pad isn't available, a ball-point pen, and last, a little observation.

STEP 1. Draw three or four squares, about one and one half

inches wide, on the paper. You can draw these squares free-hand for this experiment.

STEP 2. If you have an inked stamp pad, press the first finger, including part of the second joint, on the pad. (This finger is called the *index* finger. It is the one next to your thumb.) Roll the finger from left to right on the pad until you have a good layer of ink on it.

If you don't have a stamp pad, take an ordinary ball-point pen and rub the point of it over the tip and part of the second joint until they are entirely covered with ink.

STEP 3. Carefully, lay the inked index finger, placing the left side down first, within the square on your paper. Now, roll the finger over until it is resting on its right side. Lift the finger straight up and away from the paper. In this way you will get a clear, complete impression of your fingerprint without smudging.

STEP 4. Print *right index* underneath your fingerprint so you can identify it later.

What you have done is called *rolling* a print, exactly as would be done on a standard police or F.B.I. fingerprint card.

Practice rolling your print in the other squares until you obtain the clearest possible impression you can. You will see that a small slip can smudge a print, or too much ink can cause the lines to blur.

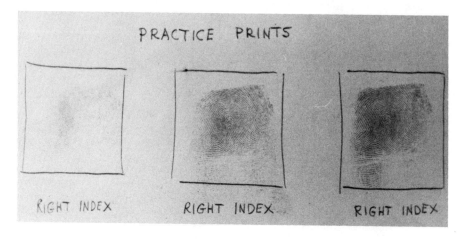

As you have seen from your first experiment, the pattern of ridge lines from your inked fingertip was transferred to the paper, just as if you had used a rubber stamp. You have observed the answer to the first question, "What is a fingerprint?" It is the *ridge pattern* found on the tips of the fingers, transferred onto another object; in this case onto the paper.

One of the advantages of experimenting is discovering more information than you were originally looking for. From observations made in your first experiment, learning what a fingerprint is, you have probably learned the answer to a few more questions:

Where is friction skin found on the body?

What is a palm print?

What is a sole print?

What are ridges?

What are furrows?

A well-trained detective, a fingerprint technician, or a crime laboratory scientist often uses the experiment method to learn the facts about a puzzling problem.

Now that you've seen what a fingerprint is and what causes it, think about the next question, "Are everyone's fingerprints really different?"

2 Are They Really Different?

Before fingerprints were accepted as a positive way to establish a criminal's identity, many methods were tried. Some of them were crude, others cruel and vicious, but none were very effective.

A thief in earlier civilizations wasn't brought into court, tried, convicted, and then sentenced to serve time in prison. Instead, he might have his hand cut off at the wrist, or maybe just a few fingers removed if the crime wasn't too serious. This way, the public would be able to recognize the thief for what he was. If the thief was unlucky enough to be caught a second time, he would have the other hand cut off. It not only served to identify him as a thief, but was supposed to prevent him from committing any further thefts.

Other criminals might be branded with a hot iron on their hands or faces, again making it easy for the public to recognize them.

Later, as cities began to expand and grow, this brutal form of identification was discontinued. The only means of identifying a criminal was by relying on memory of names and faces.

With the development of photography, identification became a little easier, but facial features change with age. It still wasn't a satisfactory method of positive identification.

By the 1850s, many scientists were already experimenting with fingerprints as a means of positive identification. William

Herschel, a British administrator in Bengal, India, was experimenting with handprints obtained from the natives. His studies over a period of twenty years led him to believe that fingerprint patterns never change during a person's lifetime.

Dr. Henry Faulds, a Scottish medical missionary stationed in Tokyo, was also experimenting and wrote papers on the subject. He corresponded with Herschel during this period and was equally convinced of the value of fingerprints for identification purposes.

English biologist Sir Francis Galton took up the study of fingerprints and wrote the first textbook on the subject in 1892. In it he described a system of classification. Though it was never used, it did serve as a basis for further research into the problem.

Working on the problem of identification from another viewpoint, a French anthropologist by the name of Alphonse Bertillon devised a new and different method. His was a complicated formula, obtained by measuring the bony parts of the body, such as the length of the arms, legs, feet, the length and width of the skull, even including fingerprints. He felt that the combination of these measurements would apply to only one adult person during his lifetime.

Though fingerprints were taken, they were just one part of the complete Bertillon formula. There was still no practical way of recording fingerprints by themselves for reference purposes.

Bertillon's method was adopted by police and prison identification bureaus as a reliable method of identification. It worked for a little more than thirty years.

Then, in 1903, a man by the name of Will West was sentenced to the United States Penitentiary at Leavenworth, Kansas.

All new arrivals at the prison were customarily photographed, and their body measurements were taken for the records, using Bertillon's system for identification.

A record clerk in the prison made the routine measurements of Will West. The measurements were reduced to a formula for filing.

In checking the formula, the clerk found another record card already on file, practically identical with that of Will West. The name on the other card was William West. The clerk asked Will West if he had ever been in Leavenworth prison before. Will West denied it.

Checking a little further, the clerk removed the photograph of William West from the files. He compared it with the new prisoner, Will West. The photos appeared to be identical. Knowing that criminals are reluctant to divulge their past records of arrest, the clerk understandably thought that Will West was lying.

The body measurements were only slightly different, which could be accounted for by normal aging. The names were practically the same, and the photos matched.

But when the clerk flipped over the record card of William West, which he had taken from the files, he realized that Will West was not lying. He saw that William West was already serving a life sentence for murder, in that very same penitentiary!

Later, when the fingerprints of the two men were compared, they didn't resemble each other at all. In checking the backgrounds of the two men, they found that Will West and William West weren't even related to each other.

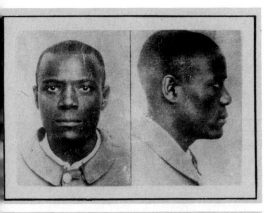

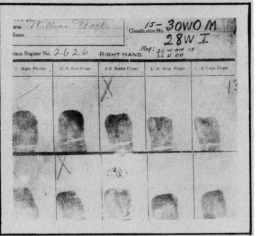
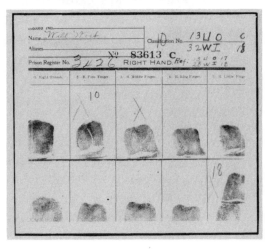

William West   Will West

This one case struck the fatal blow to the Bertillon system for identification. It clearly demonstrated the faults of relying on a system of body measurements and photographs alone. And it did serve to point out the value of fingerprints as a more reliable method.

While Bertillon's system was being widely used in France and the United States, other scientists were still working on the problem of fingerprint classification. The identification value was recognized, but the problem of classifying the prints so they could be easily recovered from a records section was still unsolved.

Sir Edward Richard Henry, the successor to Herschel's duties in India, developed an interest in fingerprints and sought a way to overcome the classification problem.

The solution came to him as he sat staring out the train window on his way to Calcutta, India. He searched his pockets for a pencil and paper to jot down the notes before his new discovery slipped from his mind. He found the stub of a pencil in his pocket, but nothing to write on. Finally, he pulled back the sleeves of his jacket, writing the notes on his stiff white shirt cuffs.

Henry based his new classification system on the previous works of Herschel and Galton. The Henry system was officially adopted by Scotland Yard in 1901, two years before the Will West case.

Interest in Henry's system of classification began to catch on in the United States. The science was first adopted by the Chief Medical Examiner of the New York Civil Service Commission, Dr. Henry DeForest, in 1902. A year later, with the Bertillon system exposed as unreliable, more and more police departments, prisons, and civil agencies began to use it themselves.

In South America, Juan Vucetich developed a different classification system in 1891. It was adopted in Central and South America, and is still being used in most Spanish-speaking countries today, as is the Henry system in most English-speaking countries.

By 1924, it was felt that a central agency should be created to handle and file all of the fingerprints being taken by police agencies, prisons, and the armed services in the United States. In that year, the Federal Bureau of Investigation created their identification division, starting with 810,188 fingerprint cards from the files of Leavenworth prison.

Today there are over 200 million fingerprint cards on file with the F.B.I. Multiply this by ten and you have over a billion single fingerprints on file, none of which has ever been found to be identical with another.

Mathematical experts claim that the chance of two fingerprints having enough identical characteristics to be identified as being the same, is beyond the realm of possibility.

As we go on to the classification and identification of fingerprints there is one point worth remembering which will help avoid possible confusion. The classification system is simply a formula derived from all ten fingers for the purpose of filing. Just as a person's medical records are filed alphabetically by name, fingerprints are filed by the classification formula.

Identification of a single print is only related to classification as a means to locate the fingerprints in the files. The identification itself is based on other means which we'll get into a little later. But for now, let's try some experiments in identifying the various pattern types, and see how they tie into the classification system.

3   Pattern Types

To understand why no two fingerprints have ever been found that are identical, we have to know about *types* and *characteristics*. The term *type* is used to identify the various fingerprint patterns. The term *characteristic* will be used later in identifying individual fingerprints.

Almost everything we can think of falls into a general type category. But when we examine an object very closely, looking for specific things about it that make it different from any other, we are examining the characteristics of that object.

Let's examine two things and observe differences.

TYPE	CHARACTERISTICS
1. A drinking glass	Glass is clear, has a chip on the rim. The chip is triangular in shape. It measures 1/2″ long by 1/4″ wide. The glass stands 3 1/4″ high. The bottom of the glass has a small air bubble in it. This is located 1/4″ in from the edge and 1″ out from the center. The bubble is shaped like a tear drop.
2. A blank sheet of paper	The paper measures 8 1/2″ × 11 1/2″. It has a small fold in the upper right-hand corner. The fold measures 1/2″ on the right edge and 1/4″ on the top edge. There is a bluish ink stain 2″

16

in from the left side. It is 5½″ from the bottom and 6″ from the top. It is shaped like a wedge.

There are millions of drinking glasses, and even more blank sheets of paper. But there is probably only one drinking glass that would have all these individual characteristics exactly as described, or one sheet of paper with a fold in the same place, an ink stain exactly in the same spot, measuring exactly the same, and having the same shape.

Before we can make a fingerprint identification from its characteristics, it is necessary to be able to identify a fingerprint pattern by type.

First let's see what type of fingerprint patterns we have in our own fingers. The only materials you will need are paper and an inked stamp pad or ball-point pen.

Step 1. This time, instead of drawing just one square, we'll make ten, in two rows of five each. The top portion of a standard official fingerprint card is divided in the same way. The squares are called finger blocks.

Step 2. Label the top row of five blocks as *Right* hand, the bottom row as *Left* hand.

Step 3. Under the first block in the top left corner, print the word *Thumb*. Under the next block to the right, print the word *Index*. The next square is labeled as *Middle*, the next as *Ring* and the last as *Little*. Label the five blocks below in the same manner, underneath each block.

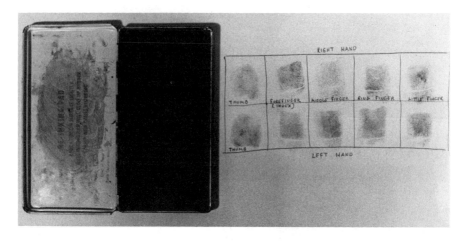

STEP 4. Starting with the right thumb, ink it on the pad, or use the ball-point pen.

STEP 5. Roll the right thumb inside the finger block you have labeled as right thumb. Next ink and roll the index finger, then the middle, the ring, and finally the little finger, all in the proper blocks you have marked. Be sure you ink and roll only one finger at a time, or you will be likely to mess up your card with ink smudges where you don't want them.

STEP 6. Ink and roll all of the fingers of the left hand the same way, again starting with the thumb.

With your rolled set of fingerprints in front of you, let's identify them by pattern type.

The first pattern type is called an *arch*. You will notice that the ridge lines seem to form a hill. They come in from one side of the pattern, rise up, and go back down again on the opposite side.

18

THE PLAIN ARCH

' Look over your set of fingerprints to see if you have any arch patterns. If you do, mark the appropriate block with a capital "A" in the top right corner, inside the block. Later, as we get into the chapter on fingerprint classification, the patterns will be marked according to their placement on the card. For now, all we want to do is to be able to identify them by type.

The second pattern type is called a *tented arch*. As you can see, it resembles the plain arch, except for one difference. Instead of all the ridge lines flowing smoothly from one side to the other, there is a sharp upthrust in the pattern, resembling a tent. Sometimes it may be just one single ridge that upthrusts, but it would make the pattern a tented arch, rather than a plain arch.

THE TENTED ARCH

Again, refer to your rolled prints and see if you have a tented arch pattern in yours. If you do, mark the appropriate block with a capital "T."

If you are not sure exactly which pattern type you have as you examine your rolled prints, read over the definitions once again. Only one pattern type is marked for each finger block.

The third and fourth pattern types are called loops. The ridge lines of the loop come in from one side of the pattern, loop around and go back out the same side.

The third and fourth pattern types are called *loops*. The large bone that projects where the wrist ends. When your hands are palm down in front of you, the "ulna" bone is on the right side of your right wrist, and on the left of your left wrist. If the loop pattern slopes toward the ulna bone, it is called an ulnar loop.

THE RIGHT SLOPED LOOP

If the loop pattern slopes in the other direction, it is called a *radial loop*, named for the radius, a less noticeable bone on the other side of the wrist.

In other words, if the loop pattern appears in a right hand

finger and the loop comes in from the right side and back out again on the right side, it is an ulnar loop.

If the lines of the loop pattern in your right hand come in from the left side, loop around and go back out the left side, it is then a radial loop.

If the ridge lines on the left hand fingers come in from the left side and go back out on the left side, they are ulnar loops.

THE LEFT SLOPED LOOP

If they come in from the right side on your left hand fingers and go back out on the right side, then they are called radial loops.

To keep it simple, just remember that loops which slope towards the ulna bone on the wrist are called ulnar loops. If they slope in the opposite direction, they are called radial loops.

Examine your fingerprint card again. If you have any loops in the right hand which slope to the right, label them as ulnar loops, marking a capital "U" in the finger block.

If you have a radial loop in your right hand patterns, mark the appropriate block with a capital "R." The radial loop on

21

the right hand comes in from the left and goes back out on the left.

Look at the patterns in your left hand. If the patterns slope to the left, mark them ulnars. If they slope to the right, mark them as radial loops.

An alternative method that is used in the classification process later is to mark loops with a line, slanting in the direction of the loop. A right sloped loop would have a slanting line to the right ($\searle$), a left sloped loop would have a slanting line to the left ($\diagup$).

The remaining four patterns are all referred to as *whorls*.

The first of the whorl type patterns is called a *plain whorl*. It resembles a whirlpool pattern or a bull's-eye. It is very easy to recognize by the spiral effect of the ridge lines.

THE PLAIN WHORL

The next whorl pattern is called a *central pocket loop*. Even though it is called a loop, it is classed as a whorl. It resembles an ordinary loop, but instead of the ridge lines coming in from one side and going out on the same side, the lines go out on the other side also.

22

THE CENTRAL POCKET LOOP

The next pattern is called a *double loop*, again called a loop, but classified as a whorl. This one too cannot be put into the loop classification because the lines do not come in and go out on the same side. If you look at the pattern closely, you will see that it resembles the letter "S" or an "S" lying on its side, or even backwards. It seems as though the lines started forming a loop, but changed their minds and went back out on the opposite side of the pattern.

THE DOUBLE LOOP

The last pattern type in the whorl group is called an *accidental*. It gets that name because that's just what it is. The pattern cannot really be classed as a loop, an arch, or any of the others though it may have similarities to one or two other pattern types.

THE ACCIDENTAL

Chances are you won't have the accidental pattern in your hand. If you do, you are one out of thousands of people.

Examine your card to see if you have any of the whorl types in your finger blocks. Mark the appropriate blocks with a capital "W." Whether it's a plain whorl, central pocket loop, a double loop, or an accidental, they are all simply marked with the capital "W."

With all of your fingerprints now identified as to type, you will see that some of the patterns are repeated. In fact it would be unusual if you had eight different patterns and only two repeats. Chances are you have mostly whorls or loops.

Look closely at two patterns which appear to be the same. Study them carefully, remembering the difference between *type* and *characteristics.*

If you believe you have two fingerprints that are exactly the same, after carefully examining them, make a check mark by them. When we get into the chapter on identifying prints and examine characteristics in more detail, maybe you'll change your mind. If not, you might be the most unusual person in the world.

For now, think about the question we asked earlier, "How does a detective at a crime scene find fingerprints that he can't even see?"

4   Latent Prints

Almost everyone knows a criminal can be identified from the fingerprints he leaves at the scene of a crime. But not everyone knows how the detective or fingerprint technician goes about finding prints he can't even see.

You know from examining your own fingerprints in Chapter 1 that there are ridge lines that form the fingerprint pattern. If you looked closely at these ridge lines you might have noticed a series of small holes in the center of the lines. These small, almost invisible openings in the skin are called pores. It is through these pores that we perspire, leaving "invisible" fingerprints on almost everything we touch. Some people's pores are more distinct than others, so don't be surprised if you can't see yours. See the enlarged illustration if you have trouble seeing them in your own fingertips.

Just as the impression of your fingerprint was transferred to the paper by inking it on the stamp pad, an invisible impression is made when we touch something because a small amount of perspiration is transferred to the object. The perspiration leaves a pattern of your fingerprint exactly as the inked impression did. The only difference is, we can't always see a fingerprint that is made in this manner. That's why it is called a *latent* print. It simply means a print is there, but it has to be made visible to the naked eye before it can be of value for identification.

The object touched doesn't necessarily have to be smooth. Identifiable prints have been brought out on surfaces such as

Note the small white dots in the ridge pattern of this accidental type print. These are the pore openings that allow us to perspire, in turn causing latent fingerprints to be deposited on everything we touch.

paper towels and even rough wood by chemical processing: using iodine fuming, silver nitrate solutions, or ninhydrin. The latter chemical reacts with the minute amounts of amino acids that are present in perspiration. Ninhydrin turns the latent fingerprint a vivid purple as it reacts, making the latent visible.

The most commonly used method, however, is *dusting*, which we'll learn about in this chapter.

Since everyone has to perspire in order to live, the detective knows there is a good chance that he can find fingerprints at the scene of a crime. Even the most experienced criminal is nervous when he commits a crime. His nervousness makes him perspire more than usual, in turn making his

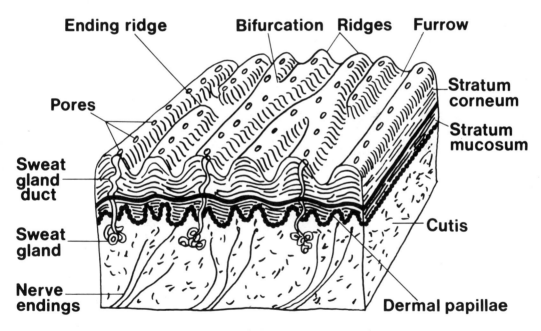

An enlarged drawing of a section of friction skin, showing the layers, ridges and furrows, and pores. Notice the dermal papillae as a double row of bumps. These are new formations of the ridge pattern being formed, in exactly the same pattern as the friction skin above, except they are in a double row at this stage, resembling a cluster of grapes.

latent fingerprints that much easier for the detective to discover.

Searching for latent fingerprints and making them visible then becomes the detective's next problem. In his mind he must try to reconstruct the movements of the criminal, thinking of objects he might have touched.

Often a criminal wears gloves to avoid leaving his fingerprints at the crime scene. But the experienced detective will search for small objects that might have been handled. He knows the criminal will sometimes remove a glove to open a small box, examine a piece of jewelry, or tear open a letter.

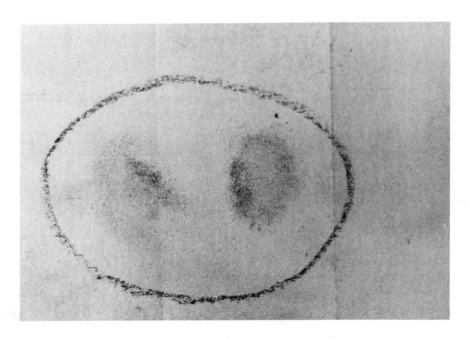

Fingerprints developed on rough paper towel using the chemical ninhydrin.

Having determined where he might find latent fingerprints at the crime scene, the detective or fingerprint technician then must develop these latents. They have to be made visible so they can be photographed and lifted.

The detective develops latent fingerprints with materials that can be found or easily made in your own home. He carries a professional kit that contains various colored powders, dusting brushes, lifting tapes, transfer cards, a flashlight, a grease pencil, evidence tags, and a magnifying glass.

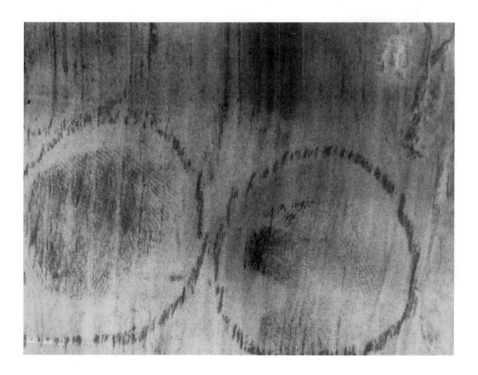

Fingerprints developed on rough section of wood using ninhydrin again.

The following will show you how to make your own finger-print kit for developing latent prints.

1. The brushes in a fingerprint kit must have very soft bristles. Otherwise they could ruin a good latent print and destroy what might possibly be the only evidence of the criminal. An ordinary watercolor brush that you use for painting is fine, but just be sure it is clean and free of paint particles. An old makeup brush that your mother or sister might not need anymore can also be used with good results.

2. Though the professional kit contains many different colored powders, the two most often used are black and gray or white. The powders are mixtures of finely ground graphite, charcoal, or lamp black for light backgrounds, and white lead or talc for dark backgrounds.

You can make your own black powder by shaving the wood from an ordinary lead pencil and scraping the lead (which is really graphite) with the edge of a knife blade. You can also substitute charcoal instead of the graphite, or try a blend of the two together.

White powder can be made from a piece of chalk, talcum powder, or even baby powder. The important thing is to use a very fine powder.

When scraping the powder, use a clean sheet of paper to do it on, then you can transfer it to a small bottle. Empty baby food jars or pill containers can be used for this.

3. The professional kit contains specially prepared tapes and lifters, but a roll of regular Scotch brand tape can be added to your personal kit. The results will be very nearly as

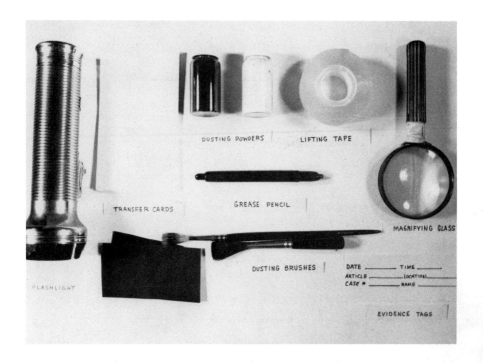

DUSTING POWDERS   LIFTING TAPE

TRANSFER CARDS   GREASE PENCIL

MAGNIFYING GLASS

DUSTING BRUSHES

DATE _____ TIME _____
ARTICLE _____ LOCATION _____
CASE # _____ NAME _____

FLASHLIGHT

EVIDENCE TAGS

good as any professional type tapes. I've used it many times myself in a pinch.

4. Transfer cards for the fingerprints in the professional kit are usually made of a slick-surfaced black or white cardboard or plastic. You can use index cards, or make your own by cutting some three by five inch pieces out of smooth white paper for the black powder lifts. For the white powder lifts, you will need black paper. Search through some old magazines for ads that have an area of black background and cut these up into small squares, large enough to hold at least one print.

5. Evidence tags of your own can be typed or printed on a

piece of paper. They should be about two inches by three inches and contain the following information:

```
DATE  5-7-74          TIME  2:05 P.M.

ARTICLE  Envelope

LOCATION  1515 Oakwood

CASE#  A-7051    NAME  RHw
```

You'll find that this is important when you've gathered a few fingerprints and try to remember where they came from a week or two later if you haven't marked them.

These tags are attached to the objects of evidence. The same information should be printed on the transfer card when the print is lifted. This way the lift and the item of evidence can be connected to each other later, and can be used to present the evidence in court.

6. An ordinary black crayon can be used in place of a grease pencil in your kit. The purpose of this is to circle and mark the developed print on the object where it is found. The grease pencil is used instead of a pen or pencil because the prints are usually found on smooth surfaces such as glass, which can't be written on in any other way. Marking it also

serves to verify that the latent print which has been lifted came from the object you say it did. When you lift the latent, you lift the grease pencil marking too. Part of the marking remains on the object, part of it is lifted, and if there is a dispute in court about where it came from, the grease markings can be easily compared to prove it came from the object of evidence.

7. A flashlight can usually be found around the home. This is used, when searching for latents, by shining the light at a very low angle to the object being examined. The latent print often becomes slightly visible, making development easier.

8. A magnifying glass is important for examining fingerprints. Check around the house. Sometimes a discarded camera lens or eyepiece can be found which will serve the purpose. Broken or discarded toys sometimes have a magnifying lens for an eyepiece. If you can't find one, it is a good idea to buy one from a variety store. They can be picked up for less than a dollar.

That completes your kit and you now have all the necessary materials to develop latent prints on many different objects.

Before we go into developing and lifting latent fingerprints in the next chapter, think about some of the things you've learned in this one. Knowing the answers is what qualifies the expert when he testifies in court.

If you were testifying on the stand, could you answer these questions?

1. What is a latent fingerprint?
2. What causes a latent fingerprint?
3. How are latent fingerprints found and made visible?
4. Why does the brush have to be made of soft hair?
5. Why is the grease pencil in the kit?

5 Developing and Lifting Latents

For your first attempt at developing latents, you'll need to set up a place to work. Whether you do the dusting on the kitchen table or on the floor, it's a good idea to spread some newspapers beforehand to do it on. It will make cleaning up afterwards a lot faster and easier.

With the newspapers spread out, and using your personal dusting kit, let's experiment on various objects. A plain, clear drinking glass, a sheet of smooth white paper, and a clean dinner plate will serve the purpose for this experiment.

Make some test impressions on the objects selected, pressing your fingers down on the plate, paper, and glass, with varying pressures from light to hard. Use different fingers also: the thumb, index, middle, ring, and little fingers.

Though a criminal at the scene of a crime isn't going to purposely leave his fingerprints for the detective to discover, it will be easier in your first attempts to deliberately make the impressions.

Next, pour a small mound of the black dusting powder into the cap of the bottle or jar you are using as a container. This prevents dipping the brush too deep into the powder and ruining a latent, and helps to keep the work area as clean as possible.

With the flashlight from your kit, direct the light beam on the glass at an angle and see if you can spot your latent fingerprint on it. Try it on the plate and on the sheet of paper. If you have a problem with this, try shining the light at different angles to the objects. You'll probably be able to see the latents on the glass and plate easily, but you may have trouble with the paper. Whether you can see the prints or not, you know they are there because you made them.

The next step is simple. Dip the dry watercolor brush into the capful of powder and spread it over the area of the latent prints. Brush the powder back and forth over the plate or glass, whichever you started with, and in a few seconds you will see the print appear, just as if you were bringing out invisible writing with chemicals.

Detective Joe Semasko dusting a clear drinking glass, using black powder. Doing the dusting over a paper towel or an old newspaper makes cleaning up afterward a lot easier.

What made the fingerprint appear? If you recall the explanation of pores and perspiration deposits on items that are touched by the fingers, you can see that it appeared because the powder stuck to this small amount of moisture on the glass. Because the glass is smooth and dry, except for the fingerprint, only the area of the print attracts the powder. You can also see how important it is for an investigator to dust for prints as soon as possible, before the perspiration deposits have had a chance to thoroughly dry out.

You have now developed your first latent fingerprints. Don't expect them to appear as clear and distinct as your inked prints. They should, however, be clear enough to distinguish the ridge lines as separate from one another. If the impressions are smudgy, you might have brushed too hard or used too much powder on the brush.

Next, try the plate and paper, remembering to brush lightly, using a very small amount of powder on the brush. With a little practice you should be able to develop good, clear fingerprints.

Once the latent fingerprint has been developed and you can clearly see the ridge detail, stop brushing. If you continue to brush too much you can wipe the ridges completely away, destroying the identification value of the print.

Try dusting some dark colored objects next, using your white powder. A dark cup or glass, black plastic handles, a dark metal box, anything that comes to mind that is dark and has a smooth surface will work fine.

When you've developed a few clear latents, the next step is marking them for evidence. Using your crayon or grease pencil, circle each print, being careful not to destroy it. Then mark your initials close to it so that they will be picked up along with your print. Put the date on the object and you're ready for the next step.

Normally, the detective would photograph the fingerprint at this stage, but we can eliminate this step and go on to the next one.

In order to prevent the fingerprint from being accidentally destroyed, it is now covered with a strip of clear, transparent tape. On small objects like the glass, plate, and paper, the tape would be left on, and the objects would be held for evidence. But suppose the fingerprint were found on the wall or a door. The detective couldn't very well take a wall or door into the station and hold it for evidence.

Detective Semasko applies a clear lifting tape over the dusted print. Though this tape is specifically made for lifting latent prints, ordinary transparent tape will do the job almost as well.

On objects that are too large to be taken and held for evidence, the print must be photographed right where it is. This is usually done with a special fingerprint camera. If the print is on wallpaper it must be left where it is. There is too much risk of tearing the paper and destroying the print to attempt to remove the tape from paper.

On other larger objects that can't be brought in and held for evidence the print is lifted. Lifting simply means it is transferred from the object onto the transfer card. The powder that was dusted over the latent print adheres to the lifting tape in exactly the same pattern that appeared on the object.

To lift the print from the glass or plate, begin by peeling off a strip of your tape about three inches long. Lay the tape carefully over the dusted print and smooth it out with your thumb until all the small air bubbles have disappeared. This way you will be sure to pick up all of the ridge detail of the print before making the transfer.

Peel the tape off the plate or glass, being careful not to let it wrinkle or fold over itself. Again lay the transferred print over the card and smooth out any air bubbles.

That's all there is to it. You have developed and lifted a fingerprint just as a detective would have done at a crime scene. Practice lifting the rest of the latents you've developed in this experiment.

Now all you have to do is fill out your evidence tags with the information showing where and when you lifted the prints and attach them to your items of evidence. The tag can be taped to the item of evidence with the same tape you used for lifting purposes.

Remember to put the same information on the transfer cards, so that a week or even a year from now you will be

Latent print developed on watch case, circled with grease pencil, initialed, and dated.

Latent print covered with lifting tape so the tape will pick up your initials and date from the article of evidence.

able to tell exactly where and when you lifted the prints, and from what object. You might even want to make up a case number for this experiment and add that to the card.

Practice on as many different objects as you can, remembering to use the dark powder on light colored objects, the white powder on dark colored objects. Try it on smooth polished wood, metal objects, painted items, plastic, leather, cardboard, mirrors, even smooth rocks. You'll soon discover which kinds of materials yield good latent prints and which don't, just as you've probably seen that hard pressure by the fingers tends to smudge the prints.

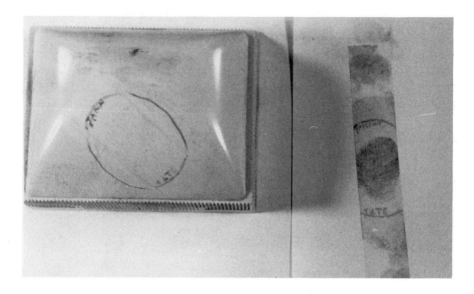

Latent print from watch case is lifted and transferred to a plain white card. Note that the grease pencil markings have been lifted right along with the print.

When you're all through dusting, and if you've done it over a piece of paper, you can save a lot of your powder for reuse. Just brush it all up into a small mound and pour it back into your container. It'll save you the trouble of making more next time.

Many people are under the mistaken impression that because he has lifted some good latent prints, the detective can identify the guilty person just from these prints. That isn't possible, except in the movies. We first must have a suspect with a card on file, or get his fingerprint card from someone who does.

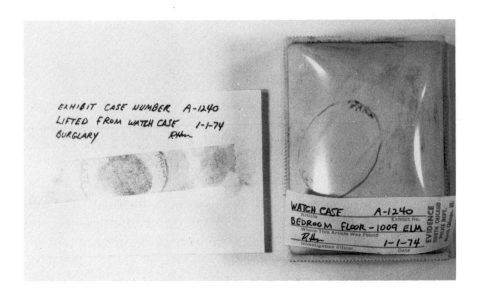

Evidence tag is filled out and attached to the article of evidence. The same information is written on the transfer card. This way the two can be identified later as being part of the same case.

This is what makes the Identification Division of the F.B.I. so valuable to law enforcement agencies. If the local police department doesn't have the suspect's card on file, there is a good chance the F.B.I. will.

With over 200 million cards on file in the F.B.I's Identification Division, finding a suspect's card could be a monumental task, especially if the suspect used a fictitious name. The following chapter should take some of the mystery out of it. You might even want to start a simplified version of your own identification bureau.

6   Classifying Fingerprints

All fingerprints fall into three general categories of arches, loops, and whorls. These are then broken down further into the plain and tented arches; the radial and ulnar loops; and the plain, central pocket, double loop, and accidental whorls.

It's easy to see that with just eight basic types of fingerprints, there has to be a method of filing the millions of recorded prints so they can be easily and quickly found. Filing them by name wouldn't be a workable plan. If a criminal wanted to hide the fact that he had been arrested and fingerprinted before, all he would have to do is use a fictitious name.

The system of fingerprint classification used today is basically the same system as that created by Sir Edward Richard Henry on the train to Calcutta. It is based primarily on pattern types, but as it goes on it gets more complicated.

However, for our purposes, we can simplify the card. Learning the primary, secondary, and small letter group within the secondary will give you more knowledge of the system than most people. With just the primary group there are 1,024 possible combinations; more than enough to start your own file. With the secondary and small letter group added to this, you can add thousands more.

LEAVE THIS SPACE BLANK	TYPE OR PRINT			SEX M	RACE Cauc.

LEAVE THIS SPACE BLANK

TYPE OR PRINT

LAST NAME   FIRST NAME   MIDDLE NAME

SMITH   John   Henry

SEX M   RACE Cauc.

HT (Inches) 69   WT 165

CONTRIBUTOR AND ADDRESS
CHIEF
POLICE DEPARTMENT
1850 LEWIS AVE.
NORTH CHICAGO, ILL. 60064

ALIASES

HAIR Brn   EYES Brn

DATE OF BIRTH 1-12-45

PLACE OF BIRTH Cal.

SIGNATURE OF PERSON FINGERPRINTED

John H. Smith

SCARS, MARKS, OR AMPUTATIONS
Ship-right forearm

YOUR NUMBER
DD 178 095

PLACE **FBI NO.** HERE

LEAVE THIS SPACE BLANK

CLASS. _____

REF. _____

SIGNATURE OF OFFICIAL TAKING FINGERPRINTS

DATE 1-15-74

REPLY DESIRED? [X] YES [ ] NO
REPLY WILL BE SENT IN ALL CASES IF SUBJECT FOUND TO BE WANTED.

1. RIGHT THUMB	2. RIGHT INDEX	3. RIGHT MIDDLE	4. RIGHT RING	5. RIGHT LITTLE

6. LEFT THUMB	7. LEFT INDEX	8. LEFT MIDDLE	9. LEFT RING	10. LEFT LITTLE

LEFT FOUR FINGERS TAKEN SIMULTANEOUSLY	LEFT THUMB	RIGHT THUMB	RIGHT FOUR FINGERS TAKEN SIMULTANEOUSLY

☆ U.S. GOVERNMENT PRINTING OFFICE : 1967—O-256-240

A standard police fingerprint card.

43

So, your card, simplified, will look like this:

CLASSIFICATION _____
LINE

1.	2.	3.	4.	5.
RIGHT THUMB	RIGHT INDEX	RIGHT MIDDLE	RIGHT RING	RIGHT LITTLE
6.	7.	8.	9.	10.
LEFT THUMB	LEFT INDEX	LEFT MIDDLE	LEFT RING	LEFT LITTLE

By referring to the card you rolled in Chapter 3, see if you can classify your own prints into their primary, secondary, and small letter classifications as we go along. Roll off a set of prints of your friends or anyone else who is willing and use them for practice.

After the prints are taken, each finger block is marked to indicate pattern types. Beginning with the index finger blocks, a *capital* letter is placed for the type of pattern in the index fingers, unless it is an ulnar loop. The ulnar loop is shown by a diagonal line, slanting in the direction of the loop.

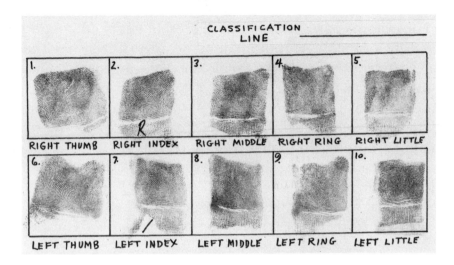

Under all of the other fingers, the appropriate *small* letter is made for every pattern except for the ulnar loop and the whorl. Again the diagonal line is used for the ulnar loop. The whorl is always marked with a capital "W."

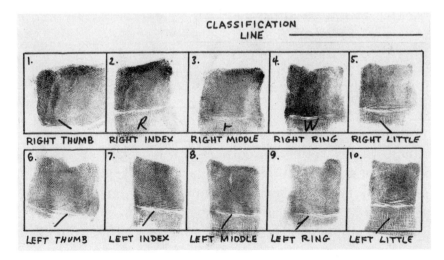

For example, an arch in either index finger would be indicated by a capital "A", but in all other fingers, by a small "a." Any pattern in the whorl family showing up in any finger would be marked by a capital "W." Any ulnar loop would be shown by a diagonal line, slanting in the direction of the loop. Radial loops would be marked with either a capital "R" or a small "r," and tented arches by either a capital "T" or a small "t," depending on whether they were found in the index or in the other fingers.

Now that the finger blocks have been marked appropriately, you are ready to learn about the classification system.

PRIMARY CLASSIFICATION

First, the fingerprints are classified according to the whorls. This is called the *primary classification*. Each finger showing a whorl pattern is given a number value.

> Fingers 1 and 2 have a value of 16
> Fingers 3 and 4 have a value of 8
> Fingers 5 and 6 have a value of 4
> Fingers 7 and 8 have a value of 2
> Fingers 9 and 10 have a value of 1

If there are no whorl patterns at all on the card, the numerical value is zero.

These values will be added together in a manner which will give you a formula. Your formula will look like a fraction, with a number on the top of the line and a number below the line. The top number is the sum of the values of the even-numbered fingers. The bottom number is the sum of the odd-numbered fingers.

One important thing to remember is that *you must add one to each sum*, when adding up the numerical values of your whorl patterns. This is to avoid confusion with the capital letter "O" and the number zero.

Therefore, if a fingerprint card had no whorl patterns in it at all, the primary classification would be written as

$$\frac{1}{1} \text{ rather than } \frac{0}{0}$$

on the classification line.

Once you have the above pretty clear in your mind, look at the *even-numbered* fingers on the sample card shown. Look for any markings for whorls, and add up their values, referring to the chart. Finger number 4 has a whorl. Its numerical value is 8 according to the chart. It is the only even-numbered finger showing a whorl pattern, so there is nothing to add in this case except the "plus one." Your sum for the top line is 8 plus 1, or 9.

Now add up the values of any *odd-numbered* fingers with

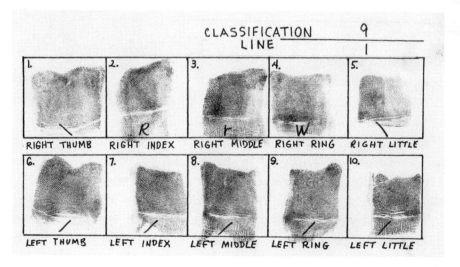

CLASSIFICATION LINE $\frac{9}{1}$

| 1. RIGHT THUMB | 2. R RIGHT INDEX | 3. r RIGHT MIDDLE | 4. W RIGHT RING | 5. RIGHT LITTLE |
| 6. LEFT THUMB | 7. LEFT INDEX | 8. LEFT MIDDLE | 9. LEFT RING | 10. LEFT LITTLE |

whorl patterns in them. You'll see that there are none. But you must still add one. Zero plus one is 1, and that goes below the line. The primary classification is $\frac{9}{1}$.

Now try classifying from your own rolled prints. First, look at the even-numbered fingers. Let's say finger number 2 and finger number 6 have whorls. Look up their numerical values, and add them together. The values would be 16 for finger number 2, and 4 for finger number 6, which equal 20. Don't forget to add one. Your sum for the top line is 21.

Now do the odd-numbered fingers. If there are whorls in numbers 3 and 7, for example, their values of 8 and 2 (from the chart) added together would be 10. Add one, your odd-number value is 11, and it goes below the line, giving you a primary classification of $\frac{21}{11}$.

With just this primary classification you can file hundreds of cards and retrieve them with no problem. It is only as the cards mount up into the thousands that it becomes necessary to extend the classification formula further.

SECONDARY GROUP

After the primary classification, the fingerprints are divided further into the *secondary group*. This indicates the pattern type of the index fingers of each hand.

It should be noted that from here on, the arrangement of the even over odd fingers is disregarded. From now on, the entries pertaining to the right hand will be written *above* the classification line, and those pertaining to the left hand *below*.

The capital letters which identify the index fingerprints on the card are inserted to the right of the primary on the classification line. The letter for the right index finger is placed above the line. The left is placed below the line. If it is an ulnar loop, the capital letter "U" is written rather than the diagonal line which is only used in the finger blocks.

Suppose the primary classification numerals were $\frac{9}{2}$ and both the left and right index fingers contained radial loop patterns. The secondary classification would then be written on the classification line as $\frac{9 \text{ R}}{2 \text{ R}}$.

If the index finger of the right hand was an arch, and the index finger of the left hand was an ulnar loop, it would be written on the classification line as $\frac{9 \text{ A}}{2 \text{ U}}$, not as $\frac{9 \text{ A}}{2 \text{ /}}$.

In our sample, the right index finger is a radial loop and the left index finger an ulnar loop. Thus, the classification now reads $\frac{9 \text{ R}}{1 \text{ U}}$.

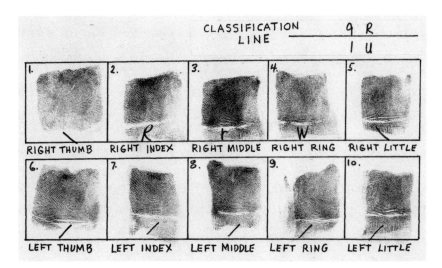

49

As you can see, this extends the filing system even more, and with each added classification it becomes narrowed down to the point where it is relatively easy to pick one card out of a group of thousands.

SMALL LETTER GROUP

You have seen that the primary classification deals with whorls, and part of the secondary classification deals with index fingers. Still within the secondary group is what is referred to as the *small letter group*, which concerns the other fingers. This is made up of prints with an arch, tented arch, or radial loop in any fingers except the index fingers. These small letter groups are inserted on the classification line in their proper positions immediately adjacent to the index fingers.

In our $\frac{9 \text{ R}}{1 \text{ U}}$ classification, a radial loop appears in the right middle finger. Since the right middle finger is immediately adjacent to the right index finger, the small letter "r" would be inserted above the line right next to the capital "R" and would look like this $\frac{9 \text{ Rr}}{1 \text{ U}}$. If the radial loop appeared in the right ring finger, which is separated from the index finger by the middle finger, a dash would be used to indicate its position. It would then look like this $\frac{9 \text{ R-r}}{1 \text{ U}}$.

If you had found a tented arch in the right middle finger, a radial loop in the left little finger, and the primary and secondary were the same as before, it would then look like this $\frac{9 \text{ Rt}}{1 \text{ U--r}}$ on the classification line.

50

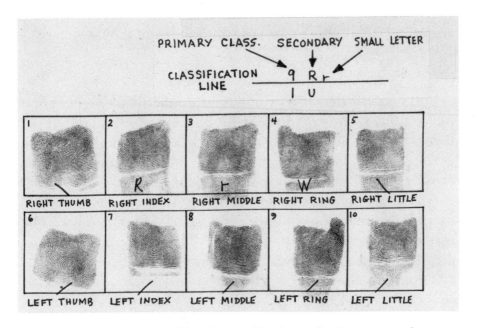

As you build up a file of classified cards they must be put in order for quick access to them. On a three by five inch index card the following information is printed: Name, date, case number, and the classification formula. This card is then filed alphabetically according to the last name.

The fingerprint cards which have already been classified are then filed according to their numerical values. All of the $\frac{1}{1}$ cards would be filed in one section, followed by $\frac{1}{2}$, $\frac{1}{3}$, all the way to $\frac{1}{32}$. All of the $\frac{2}{1}$, $\frac{2}{2}$, again, all the way to $\frac{2}{32}$, are kept separate, until you have cards all the way through $\frac{32}{32}$.

You can combine your cards so that you don't have to keep a separate section for each one, just as long as you file them according to their numerical values, from the lowest of $\frac{1}{1}$ to the highest of $\frac{32}{32}$.

You can see that if a criminal gave a fictitious name, but a police officer wanted to see if he had ever been arrested before, or was a wanted fugitive, all that he would have to do is roll a set of his prints, have them classified, and go to the classification files and compare fingerprints.

Up to this point we've only classified fingerprints according to their primary, secondary, and small letter groups. The rest of the formula contains a *subsecondary* grouping, a *major*, *final*, and *key* to complete the classification.

Though it may appear difficult at first glance, with a little practice you will be able to completely classify a card in a few minutes or analyze the type of patterns just from the classification formula.

7   More on Classification

The complete classification formula used by the F.B.I. must be carried out much further than our simplified version, in order to file the millions of cards it has on record. For you super sleuths who wish to follow the trail to the end, the complete formula follows. But if you wish to skip this chapter, or try it later, it won't affect the outcome of the projects in the succeeding chapters.

In order to understand the complete formula, we'll have to define four terms which are used in working out the classification. These terms are: *type lines, delta, innermost recurve,* and *core.*

1. The *type lines* are defined as the two innermost ridges that start parallel, spread apart, and surround, or tend to surround, the pattern area. Refer to the illustrations and the definitions will be easily understood.

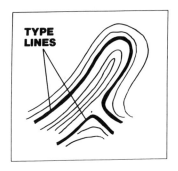
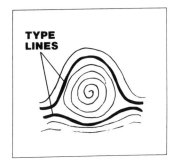

2. The *delta* is a point, located at or nearest the center, where the type lines begin to spread apart. The delta can be a dot, a short ridge, the end of a ridge, or just an imaginary point nearest the center of the diverging type lines.

3. The *innermost recurve* is the ridge line in the center of the pattern area that makes a complete loop, coming in one way, "recurving," and going back in the same direction. It is similar to the type lines described above, except it must be the innermost ridge line inside the pattern area which recurves.

4. The *core* of a fingerprint is located at a point on or within the innermost recurving ridge. It can be located on the tip of an ending ridge within the innermost recurve, or on the shoulder of the innermost recurve.

If there are two ending ridges within the recurve, the tip of the farthest one from the delta is considered the core. If there are an odd number of ending ridges within the innermost recurve, the center ridge tip is considered the core. An even number of ending ridges within the innermost recurve

would place the core on the tip of the ridge as if there were only two. That is, the second one farthest from the delta.

SUBSECONDARY CLASSIFICATION

In Chapter 6 we saw how the primary, secondary, and small letter groups are worked out. Now we can continue with the next group in the classification formula: the *subsecondary classification.*

The subsecondary classification is a further subdivision of the secondary group, but it isn't always used. Since the small letter group occurs in only about ten percent of the classifications, when they appear in the patterns the subsecondary can be dispensed with.

When no small letter group appears on the card, the subsecondary group is arrived at by the counting of ridges in the loops and the tracing of ridges in the whorl patterns. The index, middle, and ring fingers are the only ones considered in the subsecondary classification. These are fingers numbered 2, 3, 4, and 7, 8, and 9 in the finger blocks.

The *ridge count* of a loop pattern is obtained by counting the number of ridges between the delta and the core. Each ridge that crosses or touches an imaginary line from the delta to the core is counted, except for the delta and core themselves. The number arrived at in making the ridge count is then written in the top right hand portion of the finger block.

If you believe you have a loop pattern with no ridge count, refer to the explanation of pattern types in Chapter 3. You undoubtedly have a tented arch with a single upthrusting ridge, rather than a loop. To classify as a loop, the pattern must have at least one ridge count between the delta and the core.

The ridge counts of loop patterns are then converted to the capital letters "I" or "O" from the following table before they are brought up on the classification line.

Index Fingers (blocks numbered 2 and 7)
A ridge count of 1 through 9   I
A ridge count of 10 or more   O

Middle Fingers (blocks numbered 3 and 8)
A ridge count of 1 through 10   I
A ridge count of 11 or more   O

56

Ring Fingers (blocks numbered 4 and 9)

A ridge count of 1 through 13   I
A ridge count of 14 or more   O

The capital letters indicate the size of the fingers from small to large without having to write in groups of numbers on the classification line which could cause confusion.

Referring to the table, bring the appropriate ridge count up to the classification line as either "I" or "O." The right hand counts are placed above the line, the left hand counts below the line. They are grouped just to the right of the secondary classification, in the same position the small letter group would be in, if there were one.

A loop subsecondary grouping could look like this on the classification line $\frac{OII}{IOI}$. This grouping, according to the table above, tells you that the right index finger has a count of 10 or more. The right middle has a count of less than 11, and the right ring has a count of less than 14.

The left hand group (below the line) tells you that the left index has a count of less than 10, the left middle has a count of 11 or more, and the left ring has a count of less than 14.

Whorl tracing is also part of the subsecondary classification. This is noted on the classification·line with an "I," an "M," or an "O" indicating an inner tracing, a meeting tracing, or an outer tracing.

With a subsecondary formula made up of both ridge counts and whorl tracings, the inner tracing and outer tracing may be easily confused with a small or a large ridge count in the loop pattern, because both are indicated with a capital "I" and a capital "O." A little further on, when we analyze a completed card, you'll see how an inner or outer tracing can be readily distinguished from a small or large ridge count.

Whorls are traced from the left delta to the right delta. This simply means that the ridge line is followed, beginning at the left delta, moving to the point nearest or opposite the right delta. If the ridge line which is being traced ends, the tracing continues on the next ridge line below. The number of ridges between the right delta and the point where the tracing ends are then counted. If the tracing passes inside the pattern area by three or more ridges, it is designated as an *inner tracing*. If the tracing passes outside or below the right delta by three or more ridges, it is designated as an *outer tracing*. If the tracing is within the three lines, either inside or outside of the pattern area, it is designated as a *meeting tracing*.

INNER TRACING   OUTER TRACING   MEETING TRACING

Whether it's a ridge count, a whorl tracing, or a mixture of both, only the six fingers numbered 2, 3, 4, and 7, 8, and 9 are involved in the subsecondary formula. The capital letters "I," "M," and "O" are then brought up on the classification line according to the number of the ridge count in the loops (taken from the table) or the pattern of the whorl tracing.

MAJOR

The next division of the classification formula is called the *major* division. Just as in the subsecondary, if there is a small letter group already in the classification, the major is dispensed with. If there is no small letter group, the major division is brought up to the classification line just to the left of the primary classification. This division is concerned only with the thumb patterns, and only if they are ulnar loops or whorls.

Whorl tracings are brought up to the classification line just as in the subsecondary grouping as either an "I," an "M," or an "O" indicating an inner, meeting, or outer tracing.

Ulnar loop ridge counts are converted into the letters "S," indicating a small ridge count, "M," indicating a medium, or "L," indicating a large ridge count.

A separate, expanding table is used to convert the ridge counts into the "S," "M," or "L." Remember, both thumbs are used in the major division and are converted into a letter code. The right thumb classification is placed above the line, the left below the line.

To avoid confusion when using the following table, begin by converting the ridge count of the left thumb first into an "S," an "M," or an "L." Then convert the right thumb into the proper letter code.

LEFT THUMB (ridge counts)	
1 through 11	S (small)
12 through 16	M (medium)
17 and over	L (large)

RIGHT THUMB
(when the left thumb ridge count is *16 or less*)

1 through 11	S (small)
12 through 16	M (medium)
17 and over	L (large)

RIGHT THUMB
(when the left thumb ridge count is *17 or more*)

1 through 17	S (small)
18 through 22	M (medium)
23 and over	L (large)

A glance at the chart shows that you may have a ridge count of 18 in the left thumb, which would be recorded as "L," indicating a large ridge count. However, a ridge count of 20 in the right thumb would then be recorded as an "M," indicating a medium, rather than an "L." It would look like this on the classification line $\frac{M}{L}$.

As you can see from the table, the count doesn't change until it reaches 17 or more ridges, then the table expands accordingly. Another example might be a count of 20 in the left thumb and a count of 16 in the right thumb. Referring to the table, your classification should look like this $\frac{S}{L}$.

Since the thumbs are the largest of the fingers, often containing high ridge counts, this expanding table affords the classifier the opportunity to subdivide the major division still further. It allows a more even distribution of the millions of cards that must be filed, plus making retrieval of the cards a little easier by reducing the number of cards in each subdivision.

FINAL

The next classification of the formula is referred to as the *final*. This is the ridge count of a loop or whorl in the little finger of the right hand. It is placed on the extreme right above the classification line, indicated by the number of the ridge count. A count of 23 would be written as 23.

If there is no loop in the right little finger, the left little finger may be used. The final count is then placed below the line. Only if there are no loops in either of the little fingers may whorls be used. If the whorl is in the right little finger, the ridge count from the left delta to the core is used as the final. If the whorl appears in the left little finger, the ridge count from the right delta to the core is used as the final.

The ridge counts of whorls are counted from one delta only, just as though you were making a ridge count of a loop, disregarding the other delta.

A radial loop may be used as the final, but if both little fingers have an arch or tented arch, no final is used.

KEY

The *key* is the last classification appearing on the card. It is placed on the extreme left above the classification line, no matter which finger it is taken from.

The key is simply the ridge count of the first loop appearing on the card, starting from the right thumb. For example, if the right thumb has a ridge count of 14, the number 14 would be written above the classification line on the extreme left. If the first loop appearing on the card was in the right middle finger and had a count of 10, then this count would be the key, and would be written above the classification line on the extreme left.

The little fingers are not used in the key classification because they are reserved for the final. If no loops are found on the card, or the only loop is in one of the little fingers, then no key is used in the classification.

Although it may be hard to believe now, with a little practice you will soon be able to tell the pattern types of each finger on the card simply by reading the classification formula.

8   Analyzing a Classification

Knowing what types of patterns are on a fingerprint card by looking at the formula can be helpful when it comes to searching cards for a comparison. Looking for a whorl on a card with a $\frac{1}{1}$ primary group would be a waste of time. We already know that a $\frac{1}{1}$ means we have no whorls on the card.

To see exactly how this works, let's suppose we want to determine the pattern types in this classification, $\frac{5\ O\quad 9\ R\ IOO\ 18}{M\ 17\ U\ IOO}$.

To make it simple, first draw a fingerprint card on a sheet of paper, then fill in the blanks with the proper pattern type as we go along.

Since we made out the classification formula in sequence, starting with the primary division, we also begin with the primary in analyzing the formula.

We know the primary is obtained from the whorl patterns only, with the even-numbered block values over the odd-numbered block values.

Starting with the primary classification of $\frac{9}{17}$ we can refer to the value tables and see that the only even-numbered finger block on the card which could give a total value of 9 is block number four. Block number four has a value of 8, add 1 for a total of 9.

A fingerprint card titled **PERSONAL IDENTIFICATION** with the following fields:

- SEX
- RACE
- LAST NAME / FIRST NAME / MIDDLE NAME
- FINGERPRINTS SUBMITTED BY
- HT. (Inches) / WT.
- SIGNATURE OF PERSON FINGERPRINTED
- DATE OF BIRTH
- FINGERPRINTED BY
- HAIR / EYES
- RESIDENCE OF PERSON FINGERPRINTED
- PERSON TO BE NOTIFIED IN CASE OF EMERGENCY
- DATE FINGERPRINTED
- LEAVE THIS SPACE BLANK
- NAME
- PLACE OF BIRTH
- CLASS. $\frac{5\ O\ 9\ R\ I00\ 18}{M\ 17\ U\ I00}$
- ADDRESS
- CITIZENSHIP
- REF.
- SCARS AND MARKS
- See Reverse Side for Further Instructions

Fingerprint blocks:

1. RIGHT THUMB O	2. RIGHT INDEX 5	3. RIGHT MIDDLE 14	4. RIGHT RING O	5. RIGHT LITTLE 18
W	R		W	
6. LEFT THUMB 12	7. LEFT INDEX 4	8. LEFT MIDDLE 11	9. LEFT RING 19	10. LEFT LITTLE 14

LEFT FOUR FINGERS TAKEN SIMULTANEOUSLY | LEFT THUMB | RIGHT THUMB | RIGHT FOUR FINGERS TAKEN SIMULTANEOUSLY

GPO : 1962 OF—655966

Compare your analyzed card, worked out from the classification alone. It should look similar to this one.

64

No other finger block or combination of blocks could give us this total value, except block number four. So we can draw in a whorl pattern on our card in this block.

Refer to the value tables again and you will see that the only odd-numbered finger block that will add up to a total of 17 is block number one, the right thumb. Block number one has a value of 16, add 1 for a total of 17 below the line.

Draw a whorl pattern in block number one on the finger-print card. These pattern drawings don't have to be perfect, they are just for reference.

Moving from the primary to the secondary classification, we remember that blocks numbered two and seven, or the index finger blocks, make up the secondary group. From here on the fingers are classified according to the right hand over the left hand. A quick glance shows us that block number two is a radial loop and block number seven is an ulnar loop.

Draw the radial loop in block two and the ulnar loop in block number seven. So far we have four different blocks filled in on the card with the correct pattern types.

Next, we know that the small letter group is made up of arches, tented arches, and radial loops. But a glance at the classification line indicates none are present in the small letter group. We can only draw one conclusion for the remaining pattern types. They must all be ulnar loops.

We know there couldn't be any more whorls because our primary classification would be different. We know there are no arches, tented arches, or radial loops because they would have been indicated on the classification line by the small letter group. Therefore, the only pattern type remaining that will fit is the ulnar loop. Any other pattern type would have to change the classification.

Now we can fill in the remaining finger blocks with ulnar loop patterns.

With just the primary, secondary, and absence of the small letter group, we've been able to put in the pattern types of all ten fingers on the card, in the correct positions. But that isn't all we can deduce from the classification formula.

The remaining analysis is based on your knowledge from reading Chapter 7. If you skipped it earlier, you may want to go back now, or you can move ahead to Chapter 9 at this point.

Going on to the subsecondary of $\frac{IOO}{IOO}$ we can also determine which fingers are whorl tracings, which are ridge counts, and from the counts, the relative size of the fingers.

You'll recall that fingers numbered 2, 3, 4, and 7, 8, and 9 are used to derive the subsecondary formula. A look at the pattern types you've drawn in those blocks shows they are all loop patterns, except block number four. It should be clear that the blocks numbered 2, 3, 7, 8, and 9 are ridge counts, and block number four indicates a whorl tracing.

Referring to the value tables you can see that a capital "I" in the right index finger (block 2) indicates a ridge count of 1 to 9. Write this value in the upper right hand corner of finger block number two. A capital "O" in the right middle indicates a count of 11 or over, and another capital "O" in the right ring indicates an outer whorl tracing. Write these values in the upper right corners of the finger blocks.

Below the line, still in the subsecondary grouping, a capital "I" indicates a count of 1 to 9. Put this in the top right corner of block number seven. A capital "O" in the left middle finger is again a count of 11 or over, and finally the last capital "O" in the ring finger indicates a ridge count this time of 14 or over. Write these in finger blocks numbered 8 and 9.

Before working out our primary classification and placing our whorl patterns, the "O" might have been confused with a ridge count in the subsecondary group. Now we can see from our drawing that block number four referred to a whorl tracing and not a ridge count.

Moving on to the major classification (the one to the left of the primary grouping), we know this is derived from the loop or whorl patterns in the thumbs only.

We can see by looking at finger blocks numbered one and six that we have a whorl in block number one and an ulnar loop in block six, for an $\frac{O}{M}$ classification.

It's easy to see that the "O" in block number one refers to an outer tracing while the "M" indicates a medium sized thumb with a ridge count of 12 to 16. Again, put these values in the upper right corners of the finger blocks.

From the final (the number on the extreme right), we can see that we have a loop in the right little finger with a ridge count of 18. Write this in the upper right corner of block number five.

Finally, we can tell that the right index is used as the key and has a count of 5. Since finger block number one contains a whorl pattern, the first loop appearing on the card is the right index finger. Therefore, this is used as the key.

Previously we determined finger block number two as having a count of 1 to 9. But, since it was used as the key, we know the ridge count is exactly 5. We can cross out the 1 to 9 we wrote in before, and insert the 5.

From the classification alone we've been able to determine the pattern types of all ten fingers, the type of whorl tracing, and the approximate ridge count of five of the fingers and the exact count of two more.

You may want to practice classifying more cards all the way through, trying to place the patterns from the formula.

You can experiment with different classifications just by using your own fingers. Instead of rolling the prints in order, try rolling your index finger where the thumbprint would go, or your ring finger in the middle finger block. Work out as many combinations as you can.

The sample classification just worked out was done in this manner. The actual classification it was taken from is $\frac{14 \ 9 \ Rr \ 18}{1 \ U}$. See if you can analyze the pattern types just from this classification.

It should be evident now that by the use of the classification formula, millions of cards can be filed and quickly retrieved, whether a person uses a fictitious name or not.

Filing the cards is always done in the same order, just as in the simplified version earlier. Starting with the primary of $\frac{1}{1}$ through $\frac{32}{32}$, the cards are subdivided further into the secondary and small letter groups in alphabetical order, then the subsecondary and the major, with the final and the key by number.

The following chapter will deal with the identification of fingerprints from their characteristics. Many times people believe that when a fingerprint card has been classified it means a person has been identified with an unknown fingerprint. As you have seen, this isn't the case. Classification simply means the fingerprints have been coded for filing. Identification is accomplished by comparing certain basic characteristics of a single known fingerprint with an unknown fingerprint.

This is where the hunt for the elusive quarry begins, and where many crimes are solved.

9 Fingerprint Characteristics

When a fingerprint technician attempts to identify an unknown fingerprint with a known fingerprint, there are certain characteristics he must look for.

When we examined our fingerprints to see if they contained loops, whorls, or arches, we were looking at them to determine what *type* they were. Now, we are going to look within the patterns themselves for certain characteristics.

There are seven basic ridge characteristics that are used in the process of identifying one fingerprint with another. These seven characteristics are:

1. ending ridge
2. bifurcation (or fork)
3. trifurcation
4. the dot (or island)
5. enclosure
6. bridge
7. hook (or spur)

It isn't necessary, or even probable, that a fingerprint will have all seven characteristics present in the pattern. Chances are you will find no more than four or five in one finger pattern.

Look at the illustrations and you will see how the individual characteristics got their names. It will make remembering them a lot easier.

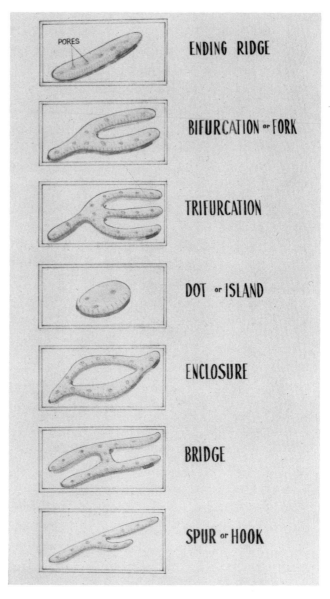

ENDING RIDGE

BIFURCATION or FORK

TRIFURCATION

DOT or ISLAND

ENCLOSURE

BRIDGE

SPUR or HOOK

The seven basic ridge characteristics used as points of reference in making an identification.

The ending ridge simply means that the ridge line ends abruptly, just like a dead-end street.

The bifurcation, though it sounds very technical, means that the ridge line had divided into two continuing lines. It is like the fork in a road. Again, this is often referred to by technicians as a fork, instead of bifurcation.

Since bifurcation means the ridge has divided into two, you have probably guessed that a trifurcation means it has divided into three continuing ridge lines.

The dot is just what the name implies. It is a small section of ridge that stands by itself like an island. In fact, some technicians refer to it as an island, rather than a dot.

Enclosures are ridge lines that divide into two lines for a short distance, but then come back again into one continuing line. Enclosures resemble the eye of a needle, greatly enlarged, or the outline of a person's eye.

The bridge is just a short ridge line that crosses and connects between two parallel ridge lines. It is just like a bridge across a river, extending from one bank to another.

Finally, hooks, or spurs as they are sometimes called, show the beginning of a fork in the ridge line, but one ridge ends within a very short distance. It might look like a road that has forked into two lines, but one of them stops abruptly.

Use your magnifying glass and study your rolled prints. See how many of the seven characteristics you are able to find in your own. You should have no problem finding an ending ridge or bifurcation. These are two of the most common characteristics found in fingerprint patterns. With some close scrutiny under the magnifying glass, you may even find four or five different characteristics in one of your fingerprint patterns.

The characteristics themselves are never marked on the fingerprint card. They are only scrutinized and used when making comparisons. Then a print is photographed and enlarged and a comparison chart made. You will see how this works in Chapter 10.

Many criminals know that these telltale characteristics are what caused their downfall and they attempt to destroy them. Some have used sandpaper to wear away the ridge detail, others have tried acid, even surgery, to change their fingerprints.

The ridge characteristics may be destroyed for a short time, but as the skin heals back again, the characteristics usually reappear in exactly the same form and position as before.

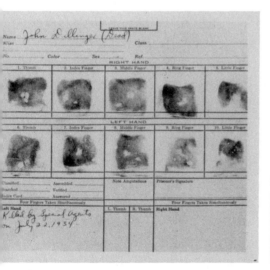 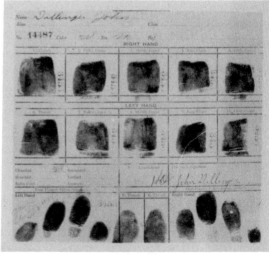

Probably the most noted attempt to destroy the fingerprint pattern was the case of John Dillinger. Still, over three hundred characteristics were found in the altered prints which corresponded to the original prints.

Sometimes part of the pattern may be completely destroyed, altering the print permanently, but usually there is still enough pattern area left to make an identification.

This distinctive pattern appears on the fingers about four or five months before a person is even born. It remains throughout a person's entire life in exactly the same pattern and detail.

During the early thirties, members of the notorious Barker-Karpis gang robbed banks, kidnapped, and murdered throughout the midwestern states. Sought by the police of these states and the F.B.I., Barker and Karpis went to an underworld surgeon. They wanted to have their fingerprint patterns destroyed by surgery. The operation was performed and a short time later, Barker and Karpis felt confident that they could never be identified again by their fingerprints. They kidnapped a wealthy brewer and banker from St. Paul, Minnesota, collecting a sizable ransom for his return.

Agents of the F.B.I. began an intensive search for clues to the identity of the kidnappers. In the search they discovered some empty gasoline cans that had been used to refuel cars in the kidnapping. One latent print of value was found, matching the right index finger of "Doc" Barker.

Arrested a short time later and put on trial, Barker glared angrily at the F.B.I. technician who explained the basics of the science of fingerprinting to the jury.

What Barker hadn't realized was the simple fact that nature restores the fingerprints to their original pattern after the skin has healed. He could have saved himself the price of pain and useless surgery. He was found guilty of the crime and received a life sentence.

Barker and Karpis were just two out of a long line that have tried to eliminate their fingerprint patterns with no success. One burglar went so far as to have a skin transplant performed. The skin from his fingertips was removed, then skin from his chest was grafted to the tips of his fingers. The process took many painful weeks to complete. It looked as though the operation was successful; there was smooth, new, pink skin on the tips of his fingers.

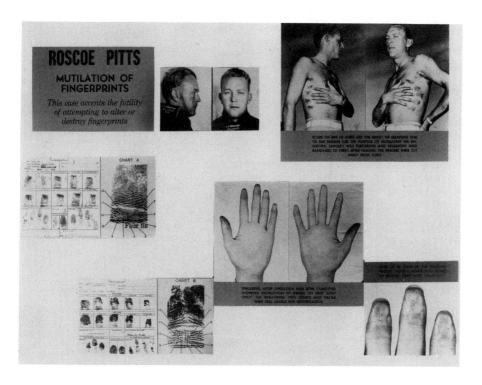

A case showing an extreme attempt to alter the fingerprint pattern. Yet, it proved unsuccessful.

Not long after, he was stopped by police as a suspicious person. Unable to produce proper identification, he was taken to the police station and fingerprinted. In a short time he was identified as being a wanted fugitive. The ridge characteristics on the sides of his fingers hadn't been completely destroyed in the transplant. Even if he had completely removed the pattern area on the fingertips, there was still enough on the second joint of the fingers to identify him.

But knowing what these characteristics are and knowing that they remain the same throughout an individual's lifetime are just the first steps. The next problem is to match the characteristics of an unknown print with a known fingerprint. You've got all the material you need right on the ends of your fingers. So let's see how it's done.

10   Making an Identification

Let's assume we're going to examine an unknown latent fingerprint and a set of inked impressions from a suspect, with the hope of making a comparison. One of the first things we must determine is whether or not the latent fingerprint matches a pattern type in the rolled prints we are examining.

Try lifting a few latents from some objects you have handled recently and see if you can compare the latents to any of your inked impressions. Try to get a set of inked impressions from other members of the family and compare any unknown latents with theirs.

If the latent print you are trying to compare is a loop type pattern, there is no use trying to compare it with an arch or whorl type pattern. It would be like trying to compare an elephant with a monkey; they're both different types.

When we've determined that the latent and one of the rolled prints are both the same type, we then search for characteristics within the pattern that are the same. This is where the magnifying glass becomes your essential tool.

One good way to start is by studying the latent print under the magnifying glass very thoroughly. Look for anything unusual in the characteristics that might help. A series of dots, an odd-shaped enclosure, or a formation of forks, all make the search a little easier. Don't hurry the examination here; it will save you a lot of time in having to refer back and forth in your beginning search.

When you've found some features in the characteristics,

Two different types of magnifying glasses used by fingerprint technicians. The one on the left is mainly used in classifying and identifying prints. The one on the right is used to examine latent prints at a crime scene to determine if they are of value or not.

examine them closely, until you can see them in your mind. You should be able to picture them as clearly as the furniture in your bedroom.

With this picture firmly implanted, check your rolled prints under the magnifying glass. Look for this distinctive feature in one of the rolled prints. Ask yourself if the characteristics match. Are they the same kind of characteristics? Are they in the same pattern area on the inked print as they are on the latent?

For example, if you were searching for three distinct dots

in a row that were on the latent print, are there three dots in a row on the rolled print? Are they in the same position as on the latent? If you found three dots on the left side of the latent, but found three dots on the top right side of the rolled print, it's not a matching characteristic. Remember, the position is just as important as the characteristic itself.

Suppose the three dots were in exactly the same place on the rolled print as on the latent. You're in luck. Now you've got a starting point to work from, in order to pick up some more characteristics.

Maybe two ridges to the left of the three dots you've spotted an enclosure. Check the latent with the rolled print exactly two ridges to the left and in the same position. Is the enclosure there also? If it is, you're making real progress now. You've got four points tagged.

Continue searching for identical characteristics in the above manner, constantly checking the type of characteristic and its position against the latent print. Do this until you have at least eight points. Though eight are sufficient, most fingerprint technicians prefer to have more. See if you can come up with a dozen or more.

Remember during your examination that the characteristics must match exactly. If you're not sure, examine them again. Ask yourself if the characteristics are all in the same pattern area on both prints. Do they match up, a fork for a fork, an enclosure for an enclosure, all the way through your eight or more points?

Sometimes, what might look like a slight difference can be accounted for in the prints. In one, an ending ridge might look like a fork in another. If the ridge lines are close together at this point, it is possible that pressure in rolling the print

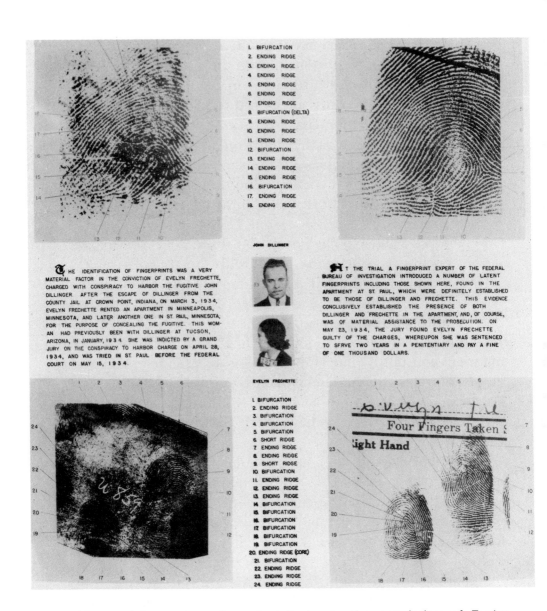

1. BIFURCATION
2. ENDING RIDGE
3. ENDING RIDGE
4. ENDING RIDGE
5. ENDING RIDGE
6. ENDING RIDGE
7. ENDING RIDGE
8. BIFURCATION (DELTA)
9. ENDING RIDGE
10. ENDING RIDGE
11. ENDING RIDGE
12. BIFURCATION
13. ENDING RIDGE
14. ENDING RIDGE
15. ENDING RIDGE
16. BIFURCATION
17. ENDING RIDGE
18. ENDING RIDGE

JOHN DILLINGER

EVELYN FRECHETTE

THE IDENTIFICATION OF FINGERPRINTS WAS A VERY MATERIAL FACTOR IN THE CONVICTION OF EVELYN FRECHETTE, CHARGED WITH CONSPIRACY TO HARBOR THE FUGITIVE JOHN DILLINGER. AFTER THE ESCAPE OF DILLINGER FROM THE COUNTY JAIL AT CROWN POINT, INDIANA, ON MARCH 3, 1934, EVELYN FRECHETTE RENTED AN APARTMENT IN MINNEAPOLIS, MINNESOTA, AND LATER ANOTHER ONE IN ST. PAUL, MINNESOTA, FOR THE PURPOSE OF CONCEALING THE FUGITIVE. THIS WOMAN HAD PREVIOUSLY BEEN WITH DILLINGER AT TUCSON, ARIZONA, IN JANUARY, 1934. SHE WAS INDICTED BY A GRAND JURY ON THE CONSPIRACY TO HARBOR CHARGE ON APRIL 28, 1934, AND WAS TRIED IN ST. PAUL BEFORE THE FEDERAL COURT ON MAY 15, 1934.

AT THE TRIAL A FINGERPRINT EXPERT OF THE FEDERAL BUREAU OF INVESTIGATION INTRODUCED A NUMBER OF LATENT FINGERPRINTS INCLUDING THOSE SHOWN HERE, FOUND IN THE APARTMENT AT ST. PAUL, WHICH WERE DEFINITELY ESTABLISHED TO BE THOSE OF DILLINGER AND FRECHETTE. THIS EVIDENCE CONCLUSIVELY ESTABLISHED THE PRESENCE OF BOTH DILLINGER AND FRECHETTE IN THE APARTMENT, AND, OF COURSE, WAS OF MATERIAL ASSISTANCE TO THE PROSECUTION. ON MAY 23, 1934, THE JURY FOUND EVELYN FRECHETTE GUILTY OF THE CHARGES, WHEREUPON SHE WAS SENTENCED TO SERVE TWO YEARS IN A PENITENTIARY AND PAY A FINE OF ONE THOUSAND DOLLARS.

1. BIFURCATION
2. ENDING RIDGE
3. BIFURCATION
4. BIFURCATION
5. BIFURCATION
6. SHORT RIDGE
7. ENDING RIDGE
8. ENDING RIDGE
9. SHORT RIDGE
10. BIFURCATION
11. ENDING RIDGE
12. ENDING RIDGE
13. ENDING RIDGE
14. BIFURCATION
15. BIFURCATION
16. BIFURCATION
17. BIFURCATION
18. BIFURCATION
19. BIFURCATION
20. ENDING RIDGE (CORE)
21. BIFURCATION
22. ENDING RIDGE
23. ENDING RIDGE
24. ENDING RIDGE

Four Fingers Taken
ight Hand

Fingerprints were an important factor in the conviction of Evelyn Frechette, charged with conspiracy to harbor the fugitive John Dillinger.

caused the ridge to touch the next ridge, making it look like a fork. Examine the end of the ridge line. Is it definitely a fork, or is there a bluntness where it appears to join, but actually doesn't?

By practicing with a latent print of your own, matching it against an inked print, you will see how differences might appear because of pressure on the ridges, or dust particles, which can also change the appearance.

Having determined that our latent print matches the inked print brings us to another problem. By examining the prints and matching the characteristics with the aid of a magnifying glass, we can see they are identical. But how do we show someone else they are identical? Suppose you had to convince a jury, or just a friend.

In the next chapter on preparing a science project, or demonstration talk, the art of making a comparison chart will show you how to convince any skeptic.

But let's recall you to the stand for a minute for some cross-examination on the subject so far. Remember, if you don't understand it yourself, you'll never convince anyone else that you do.

1. How many separate characteristics are possible in a fingerprint?

2. How many matching points are the least number needed for a positive identification?

3. What are some of the causes of distortion in a characteristic?

4. What else must we look for besides the same kind of characteristic?

5. Can you describe each of the characteristics?

11 Making a Comparison Chart

A picture is worth a thousand words, especially if you're called on to show that a latent print and an inked impression are identical. Two hours of explanation might convince someone, but one look will do the job quicker and better.

Since close-up photographs and enlargements are a necessity in preparing comparison charts, you might get a friend, or someone familiar with photography, to take your pictures for you. Maybe you've got a friend in your local police department who will take a couple of pictures with a regular fingerprint camera for you. If not, ask anyway; you might pick up some additional tips and make a friend at the same time.

If you're game, try taking your own photographs if you have the equipment. You will need a close-up lens for your camera if you don't have one. Any photo shop can help you to fit your camera with the proper close-up attachment. But unless you have the equipment, don't try taking your own. Most fixed-lens cameras cannot focus any closer than three feet. Even adjustable cameras need a close-up lens for fingerprint work.

Beside the enlarged photographs, which cost about one dollar each, all you will need for preparing your chart are: a sheet of white poster board about fourteen inches by twenty inches, a pair of scissors, a black fiber-tipped marking pen, a pencil, a ruler, an eraser, and glue.

1. Begin by placing the latent print on the right upper portion of the poster board, and the inked print on the left upper portion of the board. Find a characteristic you are going to use on the latent, and line it up so it is even with the same characteristic on the inked print.

With the prints lined up, examine them for a minute to see which parts of the excess material you can cut away. You'll want to show only the same portions of each print to eliminate any confusion that could arise if you had a completely inked impression and a partial latent print.

Trim away the excess material, realign your characteristics, then draw a light pencil outline or mark the corners so you will be able to replace the trimmed photographs in the same position for gluing.

Be sure to leave enough space between the photographs and around the sides for you to number the characteristics, and leave space at the top and bottom for lettering. The extra space at the bottom will be used to indicate the points of comparison by name.

2. Remove the photos again and glue the backs, working on some old newspaper or paper towels. A couple of spilled drops of glue can ruin the professional appearance of the chart. An amateurish looking chart doesn't inspire confidence in your ability, regardless of how accurate the comparison may be.

3. Replace the photos on the chart, making sure they are within your penciled outline and that they lie smooth and flat. Above the latent print, rule two penciled guidelines about

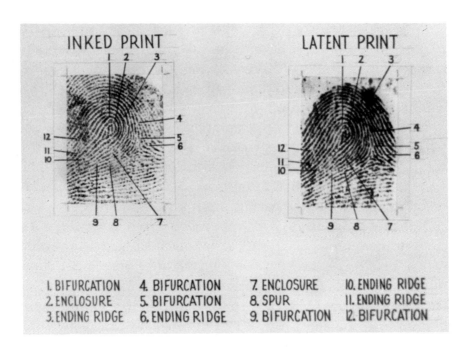

I. BIFURCATION	4. BIFURCATION	7. ENCLOSURE	10. ENDING RIDGE
2. ENCLOSURE	5. BIFURCATION	8. SPUR	II. ENDING RIDGE
3. ENDING RIDGE	6. ENDING RIDGE	9. BIFURCATION	12. BIFURCATION

A sample comparison chart.

one half inch apart. Do the same over the inked print. Again, in pencil lightly print the words, "Latent Print," in capital letters over the latent, and "Inked Print," over the inked print. Finally, draw a one half inch border around the photographs in pencil. This way when you draw out your lines of comparison they will all come out from the photograph to a uniform margin.

4. Before drawing any lines, try to work outward from the inside of the impressions to avoid crossing any lines as you go

along. Characteristics which are toward the top should have the lines drawn outward toward the top. Characteristics which are on the right should have their lines drawn out to the right; the bottom and left should have their lines out to the bottom and left. When your chart is completed, the lines will appear like spokes of a wheel, radiating out in all directions from the print.

Pick out a characteristic that is clear and distinct somewhere toward the upper inner portion of your latent print. Look back to your inked print, making sure the characteristic matches. Draw your first inked line out toward the top of the chart, stopping your line at the border you penciled in. Whether you start from the latent or the inked impression doesn't matter, as long as your characteristics are matching.

5. With your first line drawn, find the matching characteristic in the other print, drawing a line outward again at the same angle as your first line, stopping at the penciled border.

6. Return to your latent print and find the second characteristic, drawing another line from this one. Use care that you don't draw the line into the characteristic and cover it up. Draw the line just up to it, not in it. Match this characteristic again on the rolled print with a line drawn to it.

Proceed this way until you have at least twelve points of comparison matched up with lines drawn to them.

7. When you've got all your points matched, you're ready to start numbering them. You'll want this to look neat also. A simple way to do this is to rule guidelines, lightly, in pencil first.

Start at the top and work clockwise with your numbers. Rule off two lines one quarter inch apart, then pencil in number one in the space. Move to the next line, rule off two more guidelines, pencil in number two in this space. Do this all the way around the chart on both the inked and the latent print.

With all the numbers penciled in, all that's left is identifying the characteristics by name, and inking. If you have difficulty recalling the names, check back and refresh your memory.

8. Let's assume we have twelve characteristics numbered that we have to identify by name. Toward the bottom of the chart, begin by ruling off three sets of lines, one quarter inch apart, in pencil. Divide the lines into four groups for lettering. Pencil in the numbers one through twelve.

Now, referring to your enlarged photographs, see what type of characteristic you identified as point number one. For example; if it's an enclosure, pencil in the word enclosure in the space you've ruled off for number one. Move to point number two. Check for the type of characteristic again, then pencil in the name in the space for number two. Continue this until all twelve points have been identified by name.

9. Now you can go back over all your lettering and numbering with the fiber-tipped pen, trying to stay within your guidelines. Even if your lettering isn't the best, it will look neat as long as you stay within the lines.

10. Wait a few minutes until the ink has thoroughly dried

on your chart. Using a soft rubber eraser, remove the penciled guidelines. That's it, you're done. The chart is completed and should look professional.

If anyone asks you now why the two fingerprints are identical, you can explain what you've learned, pointing out the identifying characteristics as you go along. This is precisely what a fingerprint technician does when he explains to a jury what makes two fingerprints identical.

With your prepared chart, you can give a demonstration lecture to your class, Scout group, or anyone else interested in knowing more about the science of fingerprinting. You can write an explanatory paper and, together with your chart, use it as a science project. Maybe you'll just want to hang the display in your bedroom. Whatever you do with it, you can be assured that you're part of a very small group that really understands the science of fingerprinting, and how identifications are made.

12   Investigating a Crime

You've learned what fingerprints are, how to dust, lift, classify, identify, and prepare comparison charts. Now, let's see if you're ready to handle your first case from beginning to end. You're going to have to call on everything you've learned up to now. Ready?

Oddly enough, you've just finished reading the previous chapter when you get a telephone call from your best friend, Bill, the treasurer of your club. "Someone broke into the club," Bill explains. "All of the money we've saved for our baseball uniforms was stolen."

"But I thought only the guys in the club knew where you kept it hidden," you say.

"That's what I thought too, but it's gone. What are we going to do now?"

"Meet me at the club," you answer, remembering you've got a fingerprint dusting kit, itching for a trial run. Hanging up the phone, you grab your kit, checking it to make sure you've got everything in it you'll need.

A few minutes later you meet Bill in front of the clubhouse, built in a small grove of trees, hidden from view. The door is standing open, the lock torn loose from the frame.

You can easily see you're not going to get any prints from the rough wooden door. Chances are, whoever did it didn't even have to touch the door with his fingers. It looks like it was just kicked open.

"Where's the plastic money box?" you ask Bill.

"I don't know, I didn't see it around anywhere," he answers.

You know there's a good chance of picking up some latent prints from the plastic money box, if you can find it. It seems unlikely that whoever broke in would carry it very far if he didn't want to be seen with it.

"See if you can find it," you instruct Bill, setting your kit down inside the clubhouse entrance. "I'll be checking around in here. But if you do find it, don't touch it; just call me."

"What are you checking for?" Bill asks.

"Fingerprints," you answer simply.

"Fingerprints?" Bill asks, surprised. "What do you know about fingerprints?"

"Enough," you reply.

"Okay, I'll look around," he agrees, leaving.

You know the plastic money box was hidden inside another metal box, buried in the dirt floor of the clubhouse, covered with a piece of old carpet. You can see the carpet has been tossed aside, and the metal box is wide open and empty.

The only possibility for prints is on the lid of the buried metal box. Opening your kit, you pull out your flashlight, examining it for any latent prints that might be visible. You can't see any, but you know there is still a good chance there are some on it.

The metal is light gray, so you decide on the black powder to try bringing them out. Pouring a little into the cap of the container, you start brushing the surface of the lid.

Suddenly, a latent appears clearly. You remember that too much brushing could destroy the print so you stop. Circling the print with your grease pencil, you initial it, then continue dusting other parts of the lid. No other prints appear on either side of it.

Peeling off a strip of tape, you carefully place it over the latent print and smooth it out, making sure all of the air bubbles are out of it.

Bill comes rushing inside. "I found it!" he exclaims excitedly, handing you the plastic money box.

"Oh no," you groan. "I thought I asked you not to handle it."

"I forgot," he answers. "What's the difference? I found it, didn't I?"

"Never mind," you answer, knowing he has probably ruined any latents that might have been on it. "Just put it down over here."

Lifting the one latent you've brought out on the lid of the buried metal box, you transfer it to one of your cards, dating and initialing the card.

Bill stands close by, watching, fascinated now. "What's that?" he asks.

"A latent fingerprint," you explain. "Whoever broke in left a fingerprint on the lid of this box."

"But it could be mine," Bill answers. "I'm the one that handles the money for the club."

"Maybe," you answer. "But, if it's not yours, then it belongs to whoever broke in. That's what we're going to find out."

"Ah, come on," Bill grins. "You're not a fingerprint expert."

"I didn't say I was an expert," you answer. "But let's wait and see, okay?"

Dusting the plastic money box, you manage to bring out

The latent print lifted from the metal cover of the box. Can you identify it with any of the suspects' prints?

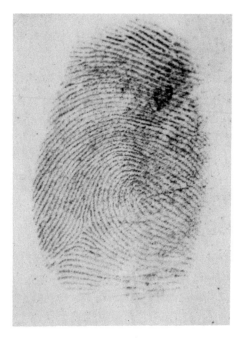

three more latent prints. But, knowing Bill has handled it, there isn't too much hope that they will be of any value.

"Hey, what's going on?" a voice asks. Jerry, Roger, and Marty, the other three members of the club, step inside.

Bill explains about the break-in and the missing money. They all seem surprised. But when Bill explains what you are doing, they laugh.

"Anybody got a better idea?" you ask.

No one comes up with any suggestions.

"Fine," you answer. "Then I'll tell you what I want all of you to do," you continue. "I'm going to make up some fingerprint cards, and I'll want fingerprints of everyone."

Showing Bill how to make up the cards, you finish lifting the latents on the plastic money box.

With the cards all prepared, you ink the tips of their fingers with a ball-point pen, rolling off a set of everyone's prints, writing each member's first name on his card.

"This is just a waste of time," Marty says as you gather up the finished cards and sit down at the small table in the center of the room.

Everyone turns to look at him, suspicion in their eyes.

"Give him a chance," Bill says. "What have we got to lose?"

"How long is this going to take?" Jerry asks. "I've got to get home soon."

"Yeah," Roger joins in. "So do I."

"Wait a minute," Bill interrupts. "Suppose you can tell who took the money by the fingerprints; what are we going to do about it?"

You hadn't really thought about that one. "Anyone got any suggestions?" you ask.

No one answers.

"Okay then, suppose we just expel him from the club, if we get the money back," you go on. "If we don't get the money, we'll go to the police with the whole story and the evidence."

Jerry, Marty, and Roger look at each other a moment, then slowly nod their heads in agreement.

Turning your attention back to the latent print, you can see that it is a right sloped loop. Glancing at the cards, you can quickly eliminate all of the other pattern types in your search.

Fingerprint cards of the three suspects, Roger, Marty, and Jerry. A hint in checking for a match: check the area of the delta in all of your right sloped loops, disregarding all other pattern types.

ROGER

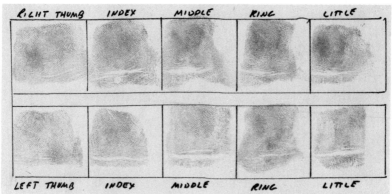

RIGHT THUMB · INDEX · MIDDLE · RING · LITTLE

LEFT THUMB · INDEX · MIDDLE · RING · LITTLE

MARTY

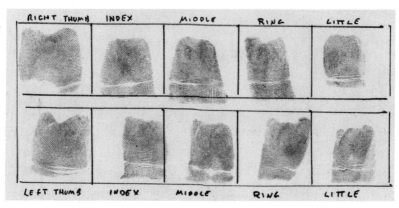

RIGHT THUMB · INDEX · MIDDLE · RING · LITTLE

LEFT THUMB · INDEX · MIDDLE · RING · LITTLE

JERRY

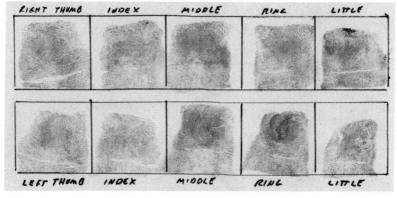

RIGHT THUMB · INDEX · MIDDLE · RING · LITTLE

LEFT THUMB · INDEX · MIDDLE · RING · LITTLE

93

Remembering that you want to look for any distinct or unusual characteristics as a starting point, you notice that there is a rather large enclosure just to the left of the delta, with a bifurcation opening up to the right of that. It looks like a wishbone lying on its side, with the two prongs pointing toward the delta.

In less than five minutes you've found the matching print on one of the suspects' cards. You turn toward him, looking him straight in the eye without saying a word. Turning red, he reaches into his pocket, draws out the club's missing money and throws it on the table, walking out without a backward glance.

Everyone is too stunned for the moment to say anything. But in a minute they are all eagerly wanting you to show them how you did it.

"It wasn't hard," you explain, showing each one how you searched for certain characteristics in the inked impressions which would match up with those in the latent, explaining how you constantly checked back and forth from the latent to the inked print until you had enough points to make a positive identification.

"I told you he could do it," Bill boasts proudly, as if he had made the identification himself.

Though it was a disappointment finding out the money had been taken by a fellow member, you feel justifiably proud. Out of the thirty different fingerprints on the cards, you found the right one and matched it correctly, picking out the guilty person.

Index

About the Author

Robert H. Millimaki has been a police officer with the North Chicago Police Department since 1958 and is currently in charge of its Detective Bureau. He has worked with fingerprints since 1962, receiving his training through the Police Training Institute at the University of Illinois from instructors furnished by the F.B.I. He first testified as an expert in an arson case a couple of years later.

During lectures to Boy Scout groups on fingerprints Mr. Millimaki noticed the avid interest they had in the subject, and that is how his book came to be.

Mr. Millimaki hopes to attend the F.B.I. National Academy, a twelve-week course offered to police officers throughout the country.